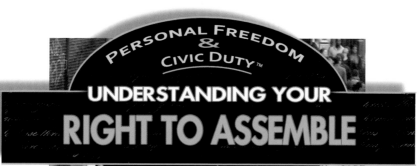

PERSONAL FREEDOM & CIVIC DUTY™

UNDERSTANDING YOUR
RIGHT TO ASSEMBLE

CAROL HAND

ROSEN
PUBLISHING®

New York

Special thanks to John and Eunice Gariglietti for consultations, encouragement, and friendship

Published in 2014 by The Rosen Publishing Group, Inc.
29 East 21st Street, New York, NY 10010

Copyright © 2014 by The Rosen Publishing Group, Inc.

First Edition

Library of Congress Cataloging-in-Publication Data

Hand, Carol, 1945–
Understanding your right to assemble/Carol Hand.
    p. cm.—(Personal freedom & civic duty)
Includes bibliographical references and index.
ISBN 978-1-4488-9461-1 (library binding)
1. Assembly, Right of—United States. I. Title.
KF4778.H36 2013
342.7308'54—dc23

2012040915

Manufactured in the United States of America

CPSIA Compliance Information: Batch #S13YA: For further information, contact Rosen Publishing, New York, New York, at 1-800-237-9932.

CONTENTS

INTRODUCTION

Should the United States be governed as a loose confederation of states with each state answerable only to itself, or should it have a strong central government with more power to control states and legislate policies affecting all states? That was the question facing the Constitutional Convention on

George Washington was the first delegate to sign the new Constitution of the United States of America in Philadelphia at the culmination of the Constitutional Convention in September 1787.

May 25, 1787, in Philadelphia. Since 1781, the United States had been a loose federation of thirteen sovereign and independent states, governed by the Articles of Confederation. But this form of government was less than successful. State economies were crashing. The weak federal government could not help—its treasury was depleted; inflation was out of control (a pound of tea cost $100 in some places); and farms were being confiscated and sold, and farmers were thrown into debtors' prison.

James Madison of Virginia was the driving force behind the Constitutional Convention. Madison felt a strong central government was the only way to save the nation. His efforts resulted in a group of fifty-five participating delegates from twelve of the thirteen colonies (Rhode Island opposed changing the Constitution and refused to send delegates). Patrick Henry also refused to attend, saying he "smelt a rat." Henry's "rat" was the decreased state power that would result from a strong central government. Henry and others felt strong state governments were necessary to protect personal liberties.

The convention lasted four months. Debates were intense and heated. On one side were the Federalists (Madison and his allies). They envisioned a government with power to regulate commerce, set commercial policy, collect taxes, support a war effort, and settle disputes between states. They were opposed by the Anti-Federalists—representatives of smaller states who feared losing the equality they enjoyed under the Articles of Confederation and southern states who feared changes in laws regulating commerce and control of slaves. After many heated battles, the delegates compromised.

The new U.S. Constitution consisted of seven articles. It described the structure and duties of the three branches of government. The first three articles cover the legislative, executive, and judicial branches. The other articles deal with amending and ratifying the Constitution and with federal versus state power. Only Article IV briefly mentions individual rights of citizens. The Constitution was signed on September 15, 1787, and ratified (signed and consented to) by the required nine states on July 2, 1788. But the vote in several states was extremely close.

The main objection was that the Constitution failed to include a Bill of Rights. Many framers thought it was unnecessary because these rights were obvious. Alexander Hamilton said that, since the government had no authority to abridge individual freedoms, those freedoms did not need to be stated explicitly. Others (including James Madison) thought freedoms were guaranteed by the checks and balances provided by the three branches of government. Thomas Jefferson disagreed. Jefferson was serving in the Foreign Office in Paris and did not attend the Constitutional Convention. But he wrote Madison that failure to include a Bill of Rights was a major mistake. According to the article "The Bill of Rights: Its History and Significance," on the UMKC School of Law Web site, Jefferson's letter said, "A bill of rights is what the people are entitled to against every government on Earth."

Anti-Federalists were so concerned that a strong federal government would erode the rights of individuals that they demanded a document spelling out specific rights such as freedoms of speech and religion. Several states refused to ratify the Constitution unless the Federalists agreed to amend it later by passing a Bill of Rights. They agreed, the Constitution was passed, and work began on the Bill of Rights. Again, James Madison took the lead. Madison's first draft was sent to Congress for revision and approval. The revised document was the Bill of Rights we know today (the first ten amendments of the Constitution). It was passed and ratified by three-fourths of the states on December 15, 1791.

T he First Amendment of the Bill of Rights outlines the individual freedoms its writers considered most essential in a free and democratic society. It consists of only forty-five words:

Congress shall make no law respecting an establishment of religion, or prohibiting the free exercise thereof; or abridging the freedom of speech, or of the press; or the right of the people peaceably to assemble, and to petition the government for a redress of grievances.

The Bill of Rights specifies those rights of individuals against which the government cannot trespass. The government has an obligation to protect those rights for every individual. No freedoms are more important that those described in the First Amendment, and no rights are more closely linked. In considering the right to assemble, we must also consider, at least briefly, the other First Amendment rights—particularly the freedom of speech and the right to petition the government for a redress of grievances. Another right, freedom of association, does not actually appear in the Constitution but has become closely intertwined with freedom of assembly.

WHAT IS FREEDOM OF ASSEMBLY?

Freedom of assembly, as guaranteed in the First Amendment, is the right of people to participate in gatherings of any kind, with people of any kind, for any purpose that is legal and peaceable. It is the only guaranteed freedom whose definition contains a qualifying word—the right to *peaceably* assemble. In other words, no one has the right to participate in a gathering if its purpose is to plot the overthrow of the government. Also, no one can form an assembly with the intention of causing violence, such as starting a riot. That is, the

In September 2012, more than twenty-six thousand Chicago teachers went on strike after failing to reach an agreement with the city on salaries, benefits, and job security. Here, teachers picket outside Wells High School.

protection of public safety overrides the right to freedom of assembly. Over the years, additional restrictions have been placed on this right. For example, permits or fees may be required for assemblies in public places. Officials may require demonstrators to follow general laws, including laws that restrict excess noise, litter, crowd congestion, or interference with traffic flow. Assemblies are also subject to laws of criminal trespass, which vary by state.

Some framers of the Constitution considered freedom of assembly particularly obvious, and

RIGHT TO ASSEMBLE AND INTERNATIONAL HUMAN RIGHTS

Freedom of assembly was first explicitly guaranteed in the First Amendment of the United States Constitution. It is now recognized throughout the world as a fundamental human right. Article 20 of the United Nations' Universal Declaration of Human Rights, published in 1948, states, "Everyone has the right to freedom of peaceable assembly and association." The same right, expressed in nearly the same words, has since been guaranteed in a number of other human rights documents, including:

- Article XXI, The American Declaration of the Rights and Duties of Man of the Organization of American States (1948)
- Article 11, European Convention on Human Rights (1950)
- Article 11, African Charter on Human and Peoples' Rights (1981)

therefore an unnecessary addition to the Bill of Rights. According to the article "The Intent of the Framers," when the bill was considered by Congress, Congressman Thomas Sedgwick wanted to strike the words "assemble and..." from the First Amendment. Sedgwick said, "If people freely converse together, they must assemble for that purpose; it is a self-evident, unalienable right which the people possess; it is certainly a thing that would never be called in question..." But Sedgwick was voted down, and the words remained in the amendment to prevent future laws from limiting the right.

ASSEMBLY VS. ASSOCIATION

Freedom of association is the right to associate with anyone you choose; that is, it protects both the composition and activities of assembled people. This freedom does not appear explicitly in the First Amendment—or indeed, anywhere in the Constitution. Yet it has become entrenched in popular, political, and legal language. Legal scholar John D. Inazu points out that, as of 2010, at least twenty-five federal district and appellate court opinions have cited a "freedom of association" clause in the Constitution, even though this clause does not exist. This is probably not surprising. David Cole, in *Supreme Court Review*, points out that, when the Constitution was written, there were no cell phones or Internet to enable communication. Therefore, the only way for people to associate was to assemble, making the two concepts virtually the same. However, Cole suggests, the framers were not interested in simply protecting the right of people to assemble. They were more concerned with protecting the "association and collective action" that assembly made possible. Thus, he feels that today's right of assembly should be interpreted as protecting people's right to associate, whether or not they are physically assembled. Freedom of speech and association are necessary for politics to exist and for individuals in a democratic society to exert control over government action. Without speech and association, individuals cannot peacefully ensure that the government remains responsive to their needs and interests. Freedom of assembly—whether that assembly involves group membership, participation in a political demonstration, or chatting over the Internet—is an integral part of this process.

Charles W. Baird, in his article "On Freedom of Association," specifically states that freedom of association is guaranteed by the freedom of assembly clause of the First Amendment. But Baird also points out that the right does not mean we are free to associate with anyone we choose because it is based on mutual consent. That is, we are only free to associate with people who also agree to associate with us. Unless this two-way agreement exists, the other person's right to

In the last several decades, freedom of assembly has been made more powerful by the Internet, which enables groups of people to communicate and organize across the country and around the world.

free association is being violated. Thus, Baird says, the word "peaceably" in this clause has two meanings— first, associations cannot use violence to achieve their ends, and second, associations cannot coerce people either to become members or to do anything against their will once they are members.

The terms "freedom of assembly" and "freedom of association" are often used interchangeably. However, legal experts usually describe association as long-term, for example, membership in an organization, while assembly refers to short-term or one-time events, such as parades or demonstrations.

WHY PEOPLE ASSEMBLE

In colonial America, assemblies were primarily political. Gatherings, often in the form of mobs that became riots, were one of the only ways poor people had to make their grievances known. These groups eventually evolved into more permanent "revolutionary associations" and later into groups with political or business-oriented goals. Assembly became a vehicle to attain social reform goals, such as abolition of slavery or the right to vote for blacks and women. Today, we continue to use assembly to further political and social goals, but we also use it to exercise "expressive" interests. Clubs and social organizations, religious groups, music and arts groups, and school or sports organizations are assemblies in which people associate to communicate and further a goal, whether it be education, socializing, or winning a game. As long as these assemblies remain "peaceable," they are legal and protected.

However, controversies arise when assemblies or associations conflict with accepted "norms" of society. Some conflicts are political. Minority or disenfranchised groups (those deprived of legal rights and freedoms) work toward equality by seeking changes in governments, societies, or organizations. They start movements, beginning with protests in the form of demonstrations, sit-ins, or other assemblies designed to get the public's (and the government's) attention. In some cases, this process may lead to profound changes in government and society. But often, the agendas of these groups are very unpopular at the beginning. This was the case for the abolitionist movement (seeking to abolish slavery), the women's suffrage movement (seeking the right for women to vote) and the civil rights movement (seeking to end segregation and secure equality for blacks). When movements succeed, as these did, the changes they bring are accepted over time. The issues do not disappear when one goal is achieved, but they evolve; new goals are developed and the issues usually become less volatile. Other groups continue to arise as well. In the first two decades of the twenty-first century, for example, the antiabortion, gay rights, and Occupy Wall

In this photo, San Francisco women join other American women, in the early twentieth century, using the power of assembly to seek passage of the Nineteenth Amendment, which would give women the right to vote.

Street movements (among others) all employed the right to assembly to further their causes.

Some issues are even more difficult than those involving equal rights. For example, freedom of speech and assembly come into question when groups promote hate, terror, or overthrow of the government—or are perceived as doing so. In these cases, rights of assembly and association sometimes become more intertwined than usual, and controversy erupts over the need (or right) of the government to limit or prohibit individuals' association with these groups. For example, do unpopular or offensive groups (such as neo-Nazis or other hate groups) have the right to have parades, demonstrations, or public meetings? Despite the

Occupy Wall Street participants march down Broadway during 2012 May Day celebrations. The movement's chant, "We are the 99 percent," voiced people's frustrations over lack of income equality.

public's general abhorrence of such groups, courts have usually upheld their rights of free speech and assembly. But this process failed in the 1950s, when the country was in the throes of the Red Scare of communism. Many people were persecuted for their membership (past or present) in the Communist Party or groups sympathetic to communism, or simply for having communist "leanings." Today's scare is Middle Eastern terrorists, not communism, but the same dilemmas exist—how much freedom do people have, based on the First Amendment, to assemble or associate with groups that might contain terrorists? Should we assume that a person is by definition a terrorist if he or she belongs to a Muslim group? Should this person, if an American citizen, have the same rights other citizens enjoy?

ASSEMBLY AND PETITION

Grammatically, some scholars consider the two rights of assembly and petition to be parts of a single right. According to author Jason Mazzone, two clues in the First Amendment language suggest this. First, the phrase states, "the right...to assemble, and to petition..." Other rights in the First Amendment are separated by the word "or"—as in "...establishment of religion....or abridging the freedom of speech, or of the press..." Second, the last clause describes "...the **right** of the people peaceably to assemble, and to petition the government...." It does not say "...the **rights** of the people peaceably to assemble, and to petition...."

Mazzone further points out that, when Madison originally drafted the Bill of Rights, he wrote separate amendments for freedom of religion, freedom of speech and press, and freedom of assembly and petition. This suggests he considered assembly and petition to be closely linked and part of the same right. The same linkage appeared in at least six early state constitutions. Only during revision were all of these rights combined into the wording that eventually became the First Amendment. According to this understanding of the clause, people have a right to assemble so they can petition for a redress (remedy or setting right) of grievances.

Other scholars, including Carol Rice Andrews, consider the rights to be more separate—that is, the right to petition belongs to individuals, as well as groups. Andrews points out that, in England, a single person could (and often did) petition the king. In fact, in 1647, the English Parliament limited the number of people who could sign a petition to twenty, and the number who could present it to the king to ten. William Blackstone's *Commentaries on the Laws of England*, published between 1765 and 1769, described the foundations of English law and provided the basis for development of American law. However, in the American edition of Blackstone's *Commentaries*

(1803), the editor pointed out, "In America, there is no such restraint." Andrews felt the framers of the Bill of Rights were more interested in "economy of language" than in making a link between the two rights. Thus, in America, although the rights of assembly and petition are closely tied to each other, the right to petition is an individual, as well as a collective, right. That is, you do not have to "assemble" in order to "petition."

THE FORGOTTEN FREEDOM?

This pair of rights, assembly and petition, are the least discussed and least studied of any explicitly stated rights in the U.S. Constitution. There are volumes written on freedom of speech, press, and religion, and on rights conferred by other amendments (for example, civil rights or the right to bear arms), but few studies have been done on the right to assemble and petition. And of the latter two, much more has been written about the right to petition. Yet both of these are essential rights of "ordinary" people—those who are otherwise powerless. These rights allow people, either individually or collectively, to demand a responsive government and to hold governments accountable for their actions.

Although the modern Supreme Court has had relatively little to say about the right to assembly (and the associated right to petition), over the years it has interpreted the clause in several ways. It has broadened the types of activities covered under this clause. Originally, an assembly was a convention such as the Constitutional Convention, and a petition was a plea by an individual to a leader, usually a king. Now, legal activities covered by this clause also include sit-ins, demonstrations or rallies, political meetings, marches, public gatherings, group boycotts, labor picketing, filing of lawsuits, and lobbying the government. The Court has also protected the right of assembly and petition for nonpolitical goals. Although influencing the government is one vital purpose of these rights, the Court views them more broadly, as part of the right of free expression. Any limitations placed by the Court on free speech also apply to petitioning. Finally, the Court has always upheld the need for assemblies to be peaceable and, when it thought them necessary, has imposed restrictions to protect public safety.

Freedom of assembly is a cornerstone of democracy and is essential to maintaining a free, open, and tolerant society. It allows people to gather and organize for all lawful purposes. According to John D. Inazu in "The Forgotten Freedom of Assembly," Abraham Lincoln once described the right of peaceable assembly as part of "the Constitutional substitute for revolution." Combined with the right to petition, assembly allows people to work actively and peaceably to influence governments and organizations

Abraham Lincoln, the sixteenth U.S. president, began the Civil War in 1861 to prevent secession of Southern states and preserve the Union, but it soon became a war to end slavery as well.

toward change. It enables groups with varying opinions and interests to freely express their issues and concerns and to take action when warranted. Thanks to the First Amendment, one of the guarantees in the United States (unlike many other countries) is the protection of free assembly.

CHAPTER 2

The Magna Carta (Great Charter) signed on June 15, 1215, in Runnymede, England, represents the dawn of democracy. It was the first written document giving citizens legal rights and protections. Previously, kings had ruled by "divine right," which meant they could do whatever they wanted because their power was assumed to come from God. After the Magna Carta, they no longer had absolute authority and had to abide by certain laws. English barons forced the Magna Carta on King John in revolt against his excessive taxation. The barons assembled to discuss their grievances, presented a petition (the Magna Carta) to King John, and backed up their demands with an armed rebellion. After the king signed the document, the barons formed a Grand Council to decide disputes, and the king had to abide by their decisions. This chapter in history showed the effectiveness of the power of assembly—of people banding together to take collective action for change.

However, the Magna Carta did not guarantee the right of assembly to later generations of English citizens. Fearing overthrow of the

New York City residents take the rare opportunity in 2010 to view the oldest known copy of the Magna Carta, dated 1217, on loan from England to the Morgan Library & Museum.

government, monarchs restricted public assemblies and jailed group members. William Penn, who later founded Pennsylvania, was arrested for public preaching in 1670 in London and charged with unlawful assembly. A judge tried to force his conviction, but a jury found him innocent. Penn's arrest and trial became a rallying point for the right of assembly in both England and America.

American colonists assumed they were entitled to the protections of the Magna Carta and English common law. Isolated from England, they developed their own assemblies with elected representatives and became almost self-governing. When British rule became more repressive under King James II and later King George III, colonists asserted their basic human rights—including freedom of assembly. They discussed, petitioned, and eventually rebelled against the unjust actions of the British government. After a long, bitter revolution, colonists freed themselves from British rule and formed a new nation. As the nation emerged, writers of the U.S. Constitution and many state constitutions took care to include peaceable assembly as a fundamental right.

ASSEMBLING FOR SOCIAL REFORM

When Thomas Jefferson wrote in the Declaration of Independence that "all Men are created equal," his statement left out more than half of the population.

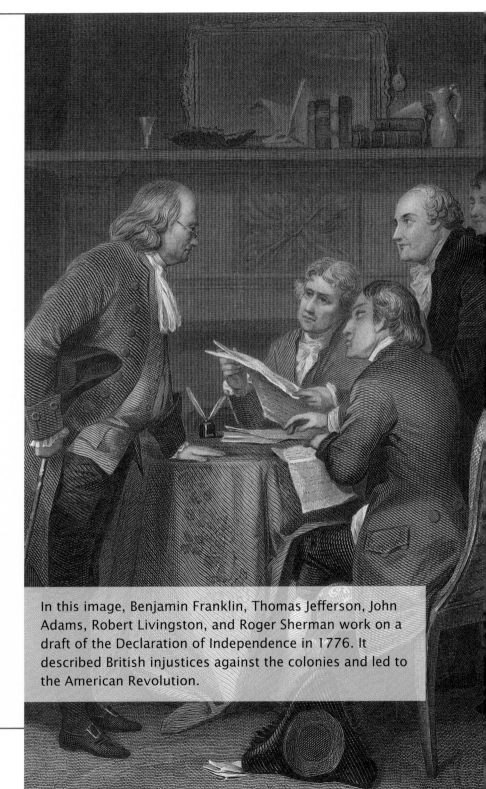

In this image, Benjamin Franklin, Thomas Jefferson, John Adams, Robert Livingston, and Roger Sherman work on a draft of the Declaration of Independence in 1776. It described British injustices against the colonies and led to the American Revolution.

He (and other founding fathers) did not intend for women, Native Americans, or African Americans—most of whom were slaves—to have the same political and civil rights as white male property owners. But people in these disenfranchised groups felt the guarantees in the Bill of Rights should apply to all citizens. Throughout the 1800s and 1900s, they founded reform movements to ensure that this happened. Reformers demanded fair and equal treatment under the law and fought for it using the First Amendment freedoms described as "freedom of expression"—speech, press, petition, and assembly.

Early activists distrusted the government and formed "voluntary associations" outside it. They felt political compromises destroyed the purity of "moral" causes such as abolition and women's rights. Reform movements expanded and strengthened as technological advances in printing and transportation made it easier to get the message out.

Abolitionists, both black and white, favored an immediate end to slavery and racial prejudice. White activists included many well-to-do women with time to devote to causes. Free blacks and escaped slaves (both men and women) became ministers and speakers, published newspapers, and helped slaves escape via the Underground Railroad. This vast, secret network of sympathizers helped over 100,000 slaves escape to the North and Canada between 1810 and

Lucretia Coffin Mott (1793–1880), a Quaker minister, was a committed social reformer and a persuasive speaker who fought tirelessly against slavery and for women's rights.

1850. But abolitionists faced stiff opposition. They were ignored, ridiculed, and subjected to violence. Antiabolitionist and anti-black mobs of otherwise respectable middle-class citizens started riots, fearing that abolition threatened their businesses and communities. In the South, groups of slaves revolted, and many were killed.

Women abolitionists quickly began to see parallels between their own situation and that of enslaved blacks. They could not vote or join men's organizations. They were not even supposed to speak in public. Women continued to fight slavery but expanded their movement to include women's rights. In 1840, abolitionists Lucretia Mott and Elizabeth Cady Stanton were refused seating at the World Anti-Slavery Convention in London simply because they were women. After many similar slights in the United States, they convened the first Women's Rights Convention in Seneca Falls, New York, in 1848. This convention released the first proclamation pointing out the similarity between the lives of women and slaves. Thus, the abolitionist and women's suffrage movements emerged nearly hand-in-hand.

Abolitionists achieved the first victories, following the great trauma of the Civil War. The Thirteenth, Fourteenth, and Fifteenth Amendments, passed shortly after the war, abolished slavery and extended citizenship and voting rights to blacks. The Fourteenth

Amendment specifically described voters as "male inhabitants," and the Fifteenth Amendment forbade denial of the right to vote based on "race, color, or previous condition of servitude." Thus, both amendments excluded women from these rights.

REFORM IN THE EARLY TWENTIETH CENTURY

In the late 1800s, several Supreme Court decisions limited freedom of assembly by linking it with petition and stating that assembly could be used only to seek remedies for wrongs imposed by the government. But citizens interpreted the freedom more broadly. During the early twentieth century, the women's movement continued with renewed vigor. Black activism expanded into a full-fledged civil rights movement. And the labor movement (also begun during the previous century) gathered momentum.

By 1908, women realized that conventions and petitions were not causing change. They began to organize parades, some with tens of thousands of participants. These parades gained press coverage and nationwide recognition. The National American Woman Suffrage Association grew from forty-five thousand members in 1907 to almost two million in 1917. Through parades, women learned and demonstrated organizational and leadership skills. And by

Alice Paul, a young Quaker woman, was fiercely committed to women's suffrage. On March 3, 1913—the day before President Woodrow Wilson's inauguration—she staged a huge suffrage parade down Pennsylvania Avenue in Washington, D.C. Resistance to the march was high and Paul feared violence, but she was promised the protection of the Washington police. Between five thousand and eight thousand brightly clad women marched, along with bands and floats documenting women's struggles with discrimination. But mobs of spectators, many of them drunken men, crashed through parade barriers and surrounded the women. They cursed, jeered, spit, pinched, and pulled at the women's clothes and banners. The parade came to a halt, while police stood by laughing and did nothing. Paul and other parade organizers finally found three cars, which they drove before the marchers, plowing a furrow through the rioting spectators. But the mob violence backfired. People around the country were disgusted by the crowd's behavior and the failure of police to stop it.

marching together, women became a cohesive force. They developed a sense of solidarity and purpose that helped them persist even when they were ridiculed, mistreated, arrested, and jailed. Finally, in 1920, the Nineteenth Amendment was ratified, and women received the vote—exactly fifty years after blacks.

Meanwhile, blacks found that equal rights under the Constitution did not translate to equal treatment in society. After the Civil War through about 1950, racist whites perverted the freedom of assembly to carry out atrocious crimes against the black population. Blacks in the South were subjected to horrific violence in the form of lynchings (brutal public murders). Northern cities had race riots, in which white mobs invaded black communities, beating and killing citizens and destroying property. Some blacks responded by arming themselves and fighting back. Others fled north. In 1909, the National Association for the Advancement of Colored People (NAACP) was founded, beginning the modern civil rights movement. The organization waged a campaign against violent attacks and against discrimination in general. But from the beginning, members of the NAACP and whites associated with their cause were considered potential threats and monitored by the FBI.

The Reverend Dr. Martin Luther King Jr., who was committed to nonviolence, led the civil rights movement from 1955 until his assassination on April 4, 1968. King's first act was to organize the Montgomery, Alabama, bus boycott. This movement to protest bus segregation in the city was galvanized by the arrest of Rosa Parks, a black seamstress. Parks had refused to move to the back of a bus to allow a white man to be seated. Under King's leadership, Montgomery blacks held mass meetings, boycotted city buses, and set up car pools to get to work. The boycott began December 5, 1955, and lasted through

Dr. Martin Luther King Jr. (*center*) and his wife, Coretta Scott King, lead the march from Selma to Montgomery, Alabama, in March 1965 to support voting rights. King was assassinated on April 4, 1968.

most of 1956. The movement came to national attention when King and eighty-eight other boycott leaders were arrested. A lawsuit, *Browder v. Gale* (1956), was filed on behalf of four Montgomery women (not including Parks). A U.S. district court found bus segregation to be unconstitutional. On November 13, 1956, the Supreme Court affirmed the district court's decision. This was a great victory, both for civil rights and for the freedoms of assembly and association in America.

In his "Letter from Birmingham Jail," King explained his reasons for nonviolent protest: "We know from painful experience that freedom is never voluntarily given by the oppressor; it must be demanded by the oppressed." A key method of nonviolent protest is civil disobedience—deliberately breaking a law to get arrested. This brings attention to unjust laws or to the cause in general and is a powerful force for change. The refusal of Rosa Parks and others to accept bus segregation was one example of civil disobedience. Sit-ins were another example. Day after day, students in southern cities protested segregation by sitting quietly at white lunch counters, even though they were refused service, until the counters closed for the day. When they were beaten by white protesters or

THE LITTLE ROCK NINE

In September 1957, nine teenagers backed by the Arkansas NAACP became the first black students to test Arkansas's segregation policy by attending all-white Central High School in Little Rock, Arkansas. Governor Orville Faubus sent the Arkansas National Guard to keep the students out, but President Dwight D. Eisenhower sent one thousand soldiers from the 101st Airborne Division to escort them into the building and protect them. The nine students returned day after day, all year. Inside the school, they were constantly shoved, humiliated, insulted, and beaten. They were prevented from sitting together in class or at lunch. White students threw firebombs and spread broken glass on the shower room floor. One student, Melba Pattillo, was stabbed, had a stick of dynamite thrown at her, and had acid thrown in her face. Only a soldier's quick action prevented her from being blinded. The teens' parents were threatened and intimidated, and four lost their jobs. But the teens and heir parents persevered, and Central High School was integrated.

arrested for "disorderly conduct," others took their place. Mass demonstrations do not break laws but are powerful forms of protest. One of the largest demonstrations in civil rights history was the August 28, 1963, march on Washington. More than 250,000 people demanding justice and equal rights for all marched from the Washington Monument to the Lincoln Memorial. There, King ended the march with his famous "I Have a Dream" speech.

LABOR AND COMMUNISM

While blacks and women struggled for civil rights, workers of all kinds struggled for higher wages, shorter workdays, safe working conditions, and other basic rights. The labor movement found the strike (ceasing work until demands are met) to be their most effective weapon. When railroads around the country cut workers' wages and simultaneously raised investors' dividends, workers staged the "Great Strike" of 1877. During this protest, more than one hundred thousand workers nearly shut down the nation's transportation system. Strikes and unrest, some violent, became more organized in 1905 with the formation of the labor union Industrial Workers of the World (IWW, or "Wobblies"). This highly confrontational workers' group organized strikes in the steel, textile, rubber, and automobile industries, among others. Masses of strikers marched in front of industry

At an IWW (Industrial Workers of the World) rally at Union Square, New York City, on April 11, 1914, a protester sports an IWW "hat card" reading "Bread or Revolution."

buildings wearing hat cards and preventing "scabs" (nonunion workers or replacements) from entering.

Russia's 1917 Bolshevik Revolution marked the rise of communism in the world and set off the first Red Scare in the United States. Leaders feared labor and civil rights movements were being influenced by communist ideas, and in the 1920s, a series of laws and Supreme Court decisions limited the right of assembly by trying to stop picketing and union organizing. But in the mid-1930s, during the Great Depression, the political pendulum swung toward unions. The National Industrial Recovery Act passed, giving workers the right to organize. Government officials spoke out, once more asserting the importance of First Amendment rights, and a key

Supreme Court decision, *Hague v. CIO* (1939), strongly endorsed freedom of assembly.

After World War II, a second Red Scare began. Hysteria about communism led to unprecedented attempts to repress basic civil rights. In 1947, President Harry Truman issued a Loyalty Order (Executive Order 9835) requiring that all federal employees be "analyzed" to determine if they were loyal to the government. The House Un-American Activities Committee (HUAC), led by Senator Joseph McCarthy of Wisconsin, targeted members of the government and the Hollywood film industry to root out "subversives," which he defined as those with leftist or communist leanings. McCarthy used hearsay and intimidation, accusing people of disloyalty with little or no evidence. Movie executives created blacklists of suspected subversives, preventing those on the lists from getting jobs.

The "McCarthy era" was an era of guilt by association. The FBI, led by J. Edgar Hoover, investigated suspected subversive activities through wiretaps, surveillance, and infiltration of suspected groups. A few actual subversives were caught and prosecuted. But the lives of many innocent people were ruined by unfounded accusations. People were watched, threatened, accused, and fired. First Amendment freedoms of speech and assembly, and particularly freedom of association, were ignored out of fear that communists would take over the country. After 1954, when the U.S. Senate finally denounced McCarthy's tactics, the Red Scare began to fade.

RECENT HISTORY OF ASSEMBLY

Since the last half of the twentieth century, U.S. protest movements have been intense, nearly continuous, and occasionally violent. After World War II, people carried out "Ban the Bomb" demonstrations for nuclear disarmament. In the volatile 1960s and 1970s, not only the civil rights movement, but also movements for women's equality and environmental protection, and particularly the anti–Vietnam War movement, took center stage.

In 1973, the *Roe v. Wade* decision guaranteed women a legal right to abortion, beginning a decades-long war between pro-choice and antiabortion ("right-to-life") advocates, which continues into the present. Somewhat later, a new civil rights movement emerged, this time fighting for LGBT (lesbian/gay/bisexual/transgender) rights. This too, has been fraught with violence, with many hate crimes directed against members of this community. Activism to stem the tide of the AIDS epidemic and care for AIDS victims began in the early 1980s. Because AIDS was originally labeled a "gay" disease, AIDS activism grew with the gay rights movement. In 1996, AIDS became more treatable when an antiviral drug cocktail was introduced. When it was no longer a certain death sentence, activism died down. But new infections did not decline in the first decade of the 2000s, and the movement is again increasing. Young people are now spreading the word through YouTube videos posted on Facebook and Myspace.

The November 1999 demonstrations at the World Trade Organization (WTO) conference in Seattle, Washington, attracted between thirty thousand and fifty thousand protesters and resulted in violence and arrests. Protesters objected to WTO policies and advocated for fair trade, labor and human rights, environmental protection, and a variety of related issues. Leaders of the protest had planned well in advance and worked out a "script" for the

U.S. Representative Louis Gohmert (Republican, Texas) speaks at a Tea Party rally outside the U.S. Supreme Court in March 2012. The Tea Party opposed the Affordable Care Act, which the Court was considering.

demonstration with the Seattle police. But some protesters failed to follow the script and violence ensued. Although most protesters remained peaceful, a few destroyed property and even briefly shut down the convention. Police resorted to nonlethal violence rather than arrests, and the mayor finally declared a state of emergency. The fiasco became known as the Battle in Seattle.

Then, on September 11, 2001, nine months after President George W. Bush took office, the United States suffered the worst terrorist attack in its history. Nearly three thousand people died in airplane attacks on the World Trade Center (Twin Towers) in New York City, and the Pentagon outside of Washington, D.C., and the downing of a jet in Pennsylvania. The aftermath included two decade-long wars in Afghanistan and Iraq, plus an unprecedented crackdown on freedoms at home in the name of security and antiterrorism. This began with the passage of the USA PATRIOT Act shortly after the attacks. Although this act contains many provisions that potentially violate the First Amendment freedoms of speech, assembly, petition, and association, few people objected to the law and it remains in effect more than a decade later. Since the passage of this act, demonstrations against the Iraq War and against suppression of freedoms at home have occurred at political conventions and elsewhere.

Most recently, during the first decade of the 2000s, a recession combined with massive unemployment and scandals in the banking and housing industries galvanized the public once again. This led to the rise of the Tea Party, an ultraconservative movement that has used both the right of assembly and political action to spread its message. The recession has also spawned the Occupy Wall Street movement of 2011, in which thousands of people occupied not only New York City's Wall Street but also parks and campuses around the country.

It is clear that people still take to the streets, parks, and sidewalks to make their voices heard, and now they also employ the Internet. But increasingly, governments' concerns for security and order take precedence over citizens' rights to express themselves and make their grievances known. The combined effect of the embarrassing Battle in Seattle and the 9/11 terrorist attacks has been to "militarize" all high-profile events where protests are likely to occur.

CHAPTER 3

THE RIGHT TO ASSEMBLE ON TRIAL

First Amendment freedoms are stated briefly in the Bill of Rights but are not explained; therefore they are open to interpretation. Sometimes conflicts arise over the exact meaning of specific freedoms, including freedom of assembly. Other conflicts deal generally with "freedom of expression," that is, some combination of the First Amendment freedoms of speech, press, assembly, and petition. When conflicts arise, courts interpret the meaning of the Constitution and amendments. They try to determine what the original framers had in mind. They read these documents and other writings of the framers and past legal experts.

The First Amendment guarantees freedom of expression to all citizens. But the type and degree of expression may be contested in court. Those losing a decision in a lower court may appeal the decision to higher courts. The Supreme Court is the final arbiter. Each court case tests the limits of a freedom.

Demonstrators both for and against President Obama's Affordable Care Act rally outside the U.S. Supreme Court on March 26, 2012. The Court was considering the constitutionality of the law, which it later upheld.

A court's decision sets a precedent (a court case cited as an example to help decide future cases). The more cases decided by the courts on a particular topic, the greater the precedent on which to draw. Taken together, the precedents describe the interpretation of a law or freedom and define its limits.

Over the years, courts, including the Supreme Court, have heard cases relating specifically to the assembly clause. These cases have related to maintaining public order and safety, use of private or public property, the civil rights of various groups, and the freedom of association. Other cases have involved freedom of expression, in which assembly

OFFENSIVE ASSEMBLIES

Some cases have tested the right of offensive groups to hold demonstrations. A famous case is *National Socialist Party of America v. Village of Skokie* (1977). This group of neo-Nazis applied for a permit to march in the town of Skokie, Illinois, whose population was more than half Jewish. Because of the Nazis' persecution of Jews during World War II, the proposed march deeply offended Skokie citizens. The Skokie Board of Commissioners tried to stop it by passing three new ordinances, which 1) required a $35,000 insurance bond, 2) prohibited distribution of printed materials promoting hatred of groups, and 3) prohibited marching in military-style uniforms. The neo-Nazis sued and the Supreme Court upheld their right to march, stating that they could not be prevented from marching based on the content of their message.

is combined with another freedom, often speech. A court can interpret a freedom broadly or narrowly. A broad interpretation increases the number of situations under which the freedom applies; a narrow interpretation limits or restricts the freedom.

AN EARLY ASSEMBLY CASE

An early Supreme Court case that limited freedom of assembly was *United States v. Cruikshank* (1876). Eight years after passage of the Fourteenth Amendment, which gave the protections of citizenship to African Americans, a white mob attacked and killed between 150 and 300 blacks (the exact number is unknown) who had gathered to defend a local courthouse in Colfax, Louisiana. A lower court convicted three men in the Colfax Massacre, but the Supreme Court overturned the convictions. The Court stated that the First Amendment "right of the people peaceably to assemble" was a right of national citizenship and assembled citizens were entitled to protection under the Fourteenth Amendment. However, it also stated that this protection applied only to encroachments by the federal government, and state governments were not required to honor it.

According to David H. Gans of the Constitutional Accountability Center, *United States v. Cruikshank* was "one of the worst Supreme Court

The Colfax Massacre (or Riot) occurred on Easter Sunday, 1873. White supremacists in Colfax, Louisiana, killed at least 150 blacks. They sought to prevent blacks from voting and restore white power.

COLFAX RIOT

On this site occurred the Colfax Riot in which three white men and 150 negroes were slain. This event on April 13, 1873 marked the end of carpetbag misrule in the South.

ERECTED BY THE LOUISIANA DEPARTMENT OF COMMERCE AND INDUSTRY 1950

decisions in American history." This interpretation of the law was extremely narrow. It ignored the due process clause in the Fourteenth Amendment, which states, "No State shall make or enforce any law which shall abridge the privileges or immunities of citizens of the United States; nor shall any State deprive any person of life, liberty, or property, without due process of law...." Since this case, several decisions have set a precedent called the incorporation doctrine. These decisions establish that, because of the due process clause, the Bill of Rights applies to state as well as federal law. Based on this new precedent, if the *United States v. Cruikshank* were tried today, the convictions in the Colfax Massacre should have been upheld.

ASSEMBLY AND PUBLIC SAFETY

Although citizens have the right to peaceable assembly under the First Amendment (and the due process clause says states cannot curtail this right), several court cases have tested this freedom. Suits have charged that protests were not "peaceable" and that protesters broke municipal laws such as disturbing the peace, disorderly conduct, impeding traffic flow, or trespassing on private property. Sometimes, arresting officers broke up peaceable protests because they feared a demonstration might lead to violence.

In the 1930s and 1940s, several labor rights demonstrations were challenged for disturbing the peace or disorderly conduct. Frank Hague, mayor of Jersey City, New Jersey, tried to suppress unions by refusing them permits, authorizing police harassment of picketers, and banning leaflets. In *Hague v. C.I.O* (1939), the Supreme Court ruled Hague's behavior illegal, stating that peaceful demonstrators cannot be prosecuted for disorderly conduct and that streets and sidewalks are public forums open to demonstrations. In *Thornhill v. Alabama* (1940), protesters that had assembled peaceably and used pickets to inform the public of a labor issue were prosecuted under state loitering and picketing laws. However, the Supreme Court ruled that they were protected under the First Amendment rights of speech, press, and assembly. In the following years, these two decisions became important precedents, upholding the right of peaceable public assembly.

But in *Cox v. New Hampshire* (1941), the Supreme Court ruled against demonstrators. Jehovah's Witnesses in the city of Manchester had to obtain a license and pay a fee for a procession down a public street. They sued, citing denial of their religious freedom. The Supreme Court ruled that such city ordinances were legal if they were "reasonable" and designed to maintain safe and orderly use of streets.

ASSEMBLY, ASSOCIATION, AND COMMUNISM

Other cases have tested the rights of people to associate with members of unpopular groups, for example, communists. Anita Whitney helped form and was active in the Communist Labor Party of California. She was convicted of teaching or advocating the overthrow of the government, and in

STUDENTS HAVE RIGHTS, TOO: THE TINKER STANDARD

In 1969, three high school students in the Des Moines, Iowa, Independent School District wore black armbands to school to protest the Vietnam War. School officials immediately enacted a "no-armband" policy, while still allowing students to wear other symbols, such as the Iron Cross. Officials said they enacted the ban because they feared the armbands would create disturbances in school. The students sued, and the case reached the Supreme Court. The Court ruled that the school had no evidence suggesting the likelihood of disturbances and that officials could not restrict student expression simply because they disagreed with it. This case, *Tinker v. Des Moines Independent Community School District*, became one of the defining cases for freedom of assembly during the Vietnam War era. It reinforced the First Amendment rights of three students, aged thirteen, fifteen, and sixteen, and became known as the Tinker standard.

Whitney v. California (1925), the Supreme Court upheld her conviction. However, it reversed the conviction in *DeJonge v. Oregon* (1937). DeJonge was convicted for conducting a meeting sponsored by the Communist Party, although he had advocated neither illegal activities nor criminal doctrines. The Supreme Court ruled that DeJonge was entitled to freedom of both speech and peaceable assembly.

According to the Illinois First Amendment Center, the Court said in part, "Peaceable assembly for lawful discussion cannot be made a crime. The holding of meetings for peaceable political action cannot be proscribed." In these two cases, the Supreme Court distinguished between peaceable and non-peaceable assembly.

In the 1950s, fear of communism led to serious attacks on First Amendment rights, thanks in large part to the actions of Wisconsin senator Joseph McCarthy. Many people were accused and many lives ruined when they were marked (sometimes with little or no evidence) as members of the Communist Party. Several Supreme Court cases upheld the rights of the accused.

ASSEMBLY AND CIVIL RIGHTS

The turbulent 1960s were filled with riots and assassinations as well as peaceful protests. Many protests, particularly in southern states, were directed against discrimination and segregation. And many peaceful protests resulted in arrests and convictions. *Edwards v. South Carolina* (1962) was brought by 187 black petitioners who had organized an antisegregation march to the South Carolina State House grounds. Although the protest was peaceful and orderly, was held in a public area,

Senator Joseph McCarthy testifies in Washington, D.C., on June 9, 1954. He is referencing a map of the United States titled "Communist Party Organization U.S.A.- Feb. 9, 1950."

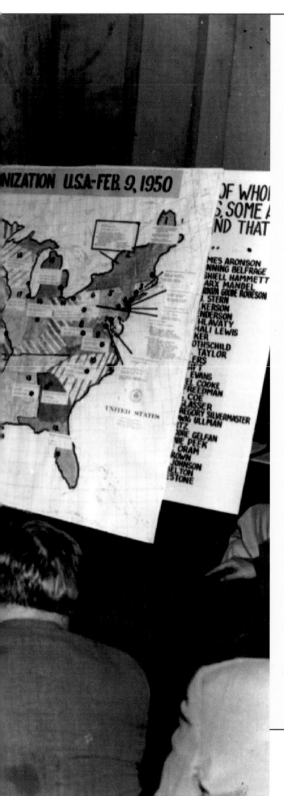

and did not block traffic, police ordered protesters to disperse. When they refused, they were arrested and convicted of breach of the peace. The Supreme Court overturned the convictions, upholding the protesters' rights of speech, press, and assembly. According to the Oyez Project, the Court ruled that a state cannot "make criminal the peaceful expression of unpopular views."

In *Cox v. Louisiana* (1964), a protester was arrested just because police feared he would incite violence. Rev.

B. Elton Cox led an antidiscrimination march of two thousand people to the Baton Rouge courthouse. During lunch hour, Cox encouraged marchers to seek service at nearby segregated lunch counters. Police dispersed the crowd with tear gas. Although marchers caused no disturbance, Cox was arrested and convicted for disturbing the peace. The Supreme Court unanimously overturned Cox's conviction, based on his right to free speech and assembly. Again, it stated that freedoms of expression cannot be denied because of hostility to a cause. In fact, the Court said, these freedoms are best used

Congress of Racial Equality members gather in Washington, D.C., on May 4, 1961, to plan the Freedom Riders march to test segregation of bus terminal restaurants and restrooms in the South.

to generate dispute, unrest, or even anger, thereby making people reconsider their preconceived prejudices. It reaffirmed this ruling in *Brandenburg v. Ohio* (1968) when Clarence Brandenburg, a member of the Ku Klux Klan, was convicted for making a racist speech at a Klan rally. The Supreme Court overturned his conviction, ruling that the Ohio law under which he was convicted violated his right of free speech.

VIETNAM AND FREEDOM OF EXPRESSION

From 1964 through 1973, the United States fought the Vietnam War. The military draft was still in effect; all young men eighteen and over could be drafted against their will, sent to Vietnam, and potentially wounded or killed—for a war many considered illegal and immoral. Protests, some violent, occurred around the country on high school and college campuses, before draft boards, and at political conventions. The most important court case involving freedom of assembly to arise from this era was brought on behalf of high school students. In *Tinker v. Des Moines Independent Community School District* (1969), the Supreme Court upheld students' right to peaceably protest the war by wearing black armbands.

SCHOOLS AND THE FIRST AMENDMENT

In the *Tinker* case, the Supreme Court upheld students' right to make a political statement within the school setting. But each case is decided on its own merits. School policy and separation of church and state also play important roles. In *Bethel School District No. 403 v. Fraser* (1986), student Matthew Fraser sued, citing the *Tinker* ruling, when he was punished for giving a student government nomination speech containing sexual references. The Supreme Court ruled against him, distinguishing between "political" speech as represented by the armbands versus Fraser's "vulgar" speech. The Court ruled that the school had the right to protect the underage student body from vulgar and offensive speech.

Several recent rulings deal with the right of students to form religious clubs on school property. These clubs are expressions of freedom of assembly, protected under the Federal Equal Access Act (1984). This act allows student-led noncurricular groups to meet on school property. It was passed at the urging of conservative Christian groups, which wanted to hold prayer meetings and Bible study groups. Largely because of this law, the number of Christian Bible clubs in public schools rose from one hundred in 1980 to fifteen hundred in 1995.

Bridget Mergens Mayhew and her attorney, Douglas Veith, leave the Supreme Court on January 8, 1990. She sought the right to hold a Christian Bible study group in Westside High School, in Nebraska.

But the law applies equally to all noncurricular groups; for example, students might meet to discuss atheism, goth culture, heavy metal music, or more recently, LGBT issues. One court case dealing with this law was *Board of Education of Westside Community School v. Mergens* (1990). Bridget Mergens sued to obtain permission to start a Christian club at her school. The Court ruled that the club could be allowed on the same basis as other student-led clubs and that this represents equal treatment, not school endorsement of religion.

According to the Bill of Rights Institute, American writer Noam Chomsky said, "If we don't believe in freedom of expression for people we despise, we don't believe in it at all." The founding fathers considered First Amendment freedoms necessary to protect minorities (those with unpopular opinions) from being silenced by the majority. However, no freedom can be taken for granted. To protect our freedoms and the citizens who use them, these freedoms must be continually tested, interpreted, and validated by the courts.

CHAPTER 4

CONTROVERSIES SURROUNDING THE RIGHT TO ASSEMBLE

In a democracy, the majority has the power and prefers the status quo, or existing state of affairs. The majority's power, economic standing, or place in society is threatened if a minority fights for and obtains equal rights. Thus, there is constant tension between majority and minority opinions. Sometimes, one side sees a moral or religious threat, as in the current antiabortion and antigay rights movements. A third situation arises when people feel their government is doing something illegal, immoral, or unjustified. This was the case, for example, with Vietnam War protests.

Controversies over freedom of assembly usually take one of two forms. First, people may object to the assembly itself. They may say it is not allowed at this place or time, is not peaceable, or interferes with normal community activities. These objections may not be easy to resolve (in fact, some require Supreme Court intervention), but they are fairly straightforward. The Constitution sets forth the "right of the people peaceably to assemble," and courts then define conditions under which assembly can occur.

UCLA students protest the Vietnam War in April 1972. Student demonstrations, many of them in California, were a major force in opposing this war.

More difficult cases arise when people object to the purpose of the assembly or the content of the protest. This type of objection is inherent in freedom of assembly because the freedom becomes necessary and is expressed only when controversy exists. It functions in cooperation with the other "expressive" freedoms— speech, press, petition, and association. Sometimes, those who object to the content of a protest may try to stop it by legally attacking the people's right to assemble. Often, violence may erupt. Both have happened—and continue to happen—in the United States.

Modern protest movements that have sparked heated controversies in the United States include the Vietnam War, the antiabortion movement, the Tea Party movement, and the Occupy Wall Street movement.

VIETNAM WAR PROTESTS

The Vietnam War (1964–1973) was the most unpopular war in U.S. history and generated massive protests around the country. Protests started small, mostly on college campuses. Leaders from the organization Students for a Democratic Society (SDS) began to educate students with a series of "teach-ins" about the war. Young people had a very personal interest in the war because nearly forty thousand young men were being drafted every month. As the war progressed, its cost and the

On July 1, 1966, an anti–Vietnam War rally in Chicago targets President Lyndon Johnson's handling of the war. Johnson did not run for a second term; he was replaced by Richard Nixon.

number of American casualties grew. Opposition mounted among the general public. In January 1967, Dr. Martin Luther King Jr., announced his opposition on moral grounds, and many returning veterans also joined the antiwar movement. By February 1968, only 35 percent of the American public approved of President Lyndon Johnson's handling of the war.

Antiwar protesters staged massive demonstrations. More than three hundred thousand turned out for a protest in New York in April 1967. On November 15, 1969, the March on Washington drew an estimated five hundred thousand people—at the time, the largest mass protest in U.S. history. But activists also relied on grassroots political organizing, congressional lobbying, civil disobedience, and draft resistance. Their anger often sparked violence. President Johnson decided not to run for reelection and was replaced by Richard Nixon, who promised a planned withdrawal from Vietnam. In February 1970, Americans first learned about the My Lai massacre, which had happened nearly two years earlier. Protesters, sickened that American troops had killed several hundred Vietnam civilians, were further enraged when, in April 1970, Nixon expanded the war by invading Cambodia. Protests escalated.

During this turbulent time, the country became more and more divided. The antiwar movement had collected many members of the dropout "hippie" counterculture, who were despised by a large segment of society. Those who favored the war considered antiwar protesters unpatriotic. They adopted slogans such as "America—Love It or Leave It," and some protesters did just that. While some young men stayed and went to jail rather than serve in Vietnam, others resisted the draft by leaving the country. These "draft dodgers" were particularly hated; they were considered cowards as well anti-American. Many antiwar activists responded by treating returning soldiers with contempt, taunting and spitting on them. More and more clashes, some deadly, occurred between protesters, police, and the general population. In 1971, the *New York Times* released the Pentagon Papers, which included extremely damaging information about the handling of the war. This was the final nail in the coffin, and the United States withdrew from the war in January 1973, leaving Vietnam still under communist control.

The Vietnam War protests were the most extensive use of the freedom of assembly in recent U.S. history. They forced people to consider the government's actions and ultimately caused political change. But the fight was long and bitter, and the country became strongly polarized. Parents were pitted against children, government against citizens, and antiwar against pro-war advocates. It took decades for the animosity to die down, and scars on society still remain.

THE KENT STATE SHOOTINGS

On April 30, 1970, when President Nixon expanded the Vietnam War by invading Cambodia, protests on U.S. campuses escalated. On May 4, Kent State students held an antiwar rally. Ohio National Guardsmen, called in by the governor, moved across the commons and ordered the students to disperse. Students reacted angrily, throwing rocks and shouting. The Guardsmen locked and loaded their weapons and threw tear gas into the crowd but did not fire. After about ten minutes, they retreated. Then, at the top of a hill, twenty-eight of the seventy-plus Guardsmen fired, most into the air but a few directly into the crowd. They killed four students and wounded nine. The Guardsmen claimed they fired in fear for their lives, and both criminal and civil trials backed up their position. But according to Jerry M. Lewis and Thomas R. Hensley, in "The May 4 Shootings at Kent State University," others agree with the Scranton Commission, which concluded, "The indiscriminate firing of rifles into a crowd of students and the deaths that followed were unnecessary, unwarranted, and inexcusable." Questions remain: did university officials respond appropriately to the demonstrations? Should Guardsmen have been called to Kent State? Who was ultimately responsible?

THE ANTIABORTION MOVEMENT

One of the most polarizing issues to arise in the last century is the abortion controversy. When *Roe v. Wade* was decided in 1973, its proponents saw it as a victory for women's rights. It was an extension of reproductive rights such as birth control, which enabled women to plan the size of their families and spacing of children. Abortion gave women control over their bodies; for example, they were no longer forced to carry a child of rape or incest. However, opponents saw abortion as legalized murder and vowed to fight until it was made illegal again. They made it a moral or religious issue, rather than one of medical or personal rights.

In their zeal to overturn *Roe v. Wade*, antiabortion activists have used their power of assembly extensively to picket reproductive health clinics and harass abortion providers and clients at health clinics. In *Scheidler v. National Organization for Women* (2006), the Supreme Court upheld the right of antiabortion activists to carry out these protests. NOW had claimed the protesters were committing extortion by preventing women from seeking medical services and doctors from performing their jobs. The Supreme Court ruled that no extortion occurred because protesters obtained no property by demonstrating. Freedom of assembly was not discussed, but the decision implicitly upholds it.

Many people feel antiabortion activists often overstep the bounds of "peaceable assembly" by using offensive and sometimes violent tactics. These have included bombing abortion clinics, rock throwing, intimidation of people entering clinics, and distributing "Wanted" posters of abortion doctors (with

Antiabortion activists demonstrate outside a Planned Parenthood clinic in Washington, D.C., on July 28, 2005. The group had walked from Maine, demonstrating at pro-choice clinics along the way.

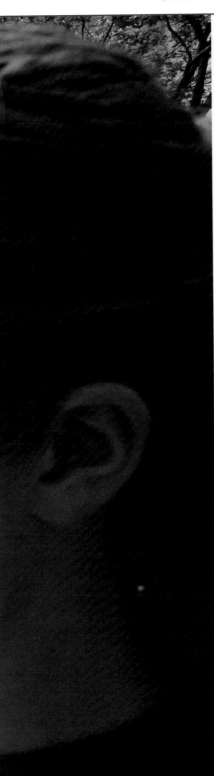

contact information) at rallies and online. Several of these doctors were then murdered, including Dr. David Gunn in Pensacola, Florida (1993) and Dr. George Tiller in Wichita, Kansas (2009).

The antiabortion movement has become increasingly radical. In 2010, many antiabortion activists were elected to state and national legislatures. In 2012, Congress introduced more than forty bills and state legislatures introduced more than six hundred bills that would limit abortion and other reproductive rights, including family planning services and, in some states, birth control itself. Now, women concerned about keeping these reproductive rights are organizing in opposition to antiabortionists. The controversy continues.

TEA PARTY AND OCCUPY WALL STREET

Since the 2008 elections, two competing movements show that freedom of assembly is still alive and well. The antitax, anti-big-government Tea Party movement officially began January 19, 2009, with an online suggestion that people mail tea bags to members of Congress. The movement spread rapidly through Twitter, Facebook, conservative bloggers, and Web sites. Members coordinated demonstrations around the country. The Tea Party first opposed the Obama administration's proposed economic stimulus package, the American Recovery and Reinvestment Act. They said the stimulus increased spending, bailed out undeserving companies, and raised the national debt. Later, they opposed

Tea Partier Dolores Harrell wears tea bags on her hat at the Restoring America rally held in Indianola, Iowa, on September 3, 2011. Former vice presidential candidate Sarah Palin spoke at the rally.

President Obama's health care reform bill, the Affordable Care Act.

The Tea Party is associated with radical, ultraconservative Republicans and also includes libertarians, social and religious conservatives, and antitax people. They have quickly become a political force. Sarah Palin, the 2008 Republican vice presidential nominee, allied herself with the Tea Party. In 2010, they elected twenty-eight new members to the House of Representatives. In 2012, Republicans chose Paul Ryan as their vice presidential nominee. Ryan does not call himself a Tea Party member, but he embraces at least some of their political views.

Other disaffected Americans ally themselves with the left-wing Occupy Wall Street movement. This movement was inspired by Occupy movements in Egypt and Tunisia, where citizens mobilized to unseat repressive dictators. Its stated goal was to fight the power of major banks and multinational corporations, which it considered responsible for the economic recession. Members of Occupy Wall Street rejected leaders and opted for collective decision-making through a "people's assembly." The movement began on September 17, 2011, on New York's Wall Street, where thousands of people occupied areas around the U.S. Stock Exchange. It quickly spread to more than one hundred other cities. It popularized the division of Americans into the "99 percent" (people without money or power) and the 1 percent (the extremely wealthy few who control the 99 percent).

People in both movements are worried about the economy and feel that large institutions ignore the wishes and needs of "little people." But they differ in whom they blame. Occupiers blame banks and the super-rich. Tea Partiers blame the government and see the super-rich as "job creators"—the solution, not the cause, of economic problems. The Tea Party favors less regulation of banks and other institutions; the Occupy movement favors more. They also differ in their methods. The Tea Party movement chose to work within the system and so far has been very successful in electing political candidates and moving the Republican Party farther right. The Occupy movement, which is nearly three years younger, chose to work outside the system. It has many locally active groups and several Web sites. But so far it has not been a major influence on the Democratic Party, the party most sympathetic to its agenda.

Freedom of assembly is valuable in a democracy because it shines a light on society's current attitudes. It enables people to make diverse ideas and opinions known and makes them think about issues in different ways. For example, if people want to stop a hate group from demonstrating, they must first stop and ask themselves, "What if we were the minority and those in power stopped us from demonstrating?"

THE RIGHT TO ASSEMBLE: PRESENT AND FUTURE

What happens when freedom of assembly is no longer considered important, or when it is prevented or so curtailed it becomes ineffective? In the late twentieth and early twenty-first centuries, we have begun to find out, with the development of two alarming trends. First, freedom of assembly is now rarely used as a basis for court decisions. Instead, decisions are based on laws unrelated to First Amendment rights or on the more elusive "freedom of association." Second, the rise of so-called free-speech zones means today's protest demonstrations are much more highly controlled than previously. In contrast to these two anti-assembly trends, the rise of the Internet in some ways makes assembly easier. But can the Internet overcome today's assaults (deliberate or otherwise) on freedom of assembly?

THE FORGOTTEN FREEDOM OF ASSEMBLY

John D. Inazu, in his 2010 article, "The Forgotten Freedom of Assembly," notes that,

Fenced off in the DZ, or "free-speech zone," far from the action, a protester identified as "Dennis" speaks on July 27, 2004, during the Democratic National Convention in Boston, Massachusetts.

although once considered a basic freedom, "in the past thirty years, the freedom of assembly has been reduced to a historical footnote in American political theory and law." During this time, very few cases based on freedom of assembly have been tried and ruled on by the courts. Courts now consider assembly only in cases of protests and demonstrations, if at all. Even these are sometimes resolved without mentioning assembly. *Boos v. Barry* (1988) challenged a District of Columbia law prohibiting "congregating within 500 feet of any building or premises of the District of Columbia used or occupied by any foreign government." The challenger cited infringement of free speech and assembly rights, but the case was decided on the basis of free speech alone, without considering assembly.

Instead of assembly, the Supreme Court formulated the concept of "freedom of association," first in regard to Communist Party members and later in civil rights cases, such as those involving NAACP membership. Inazu feels this change from freedom of assembly to freedom of association is being used to control rather than to protect the people. In making decisions, he says, judges have forgotten that freedom of assembly exists to enable groups to challenge existing values and express dissident viewpoints. He quotes C. Edwin Baker: "The constitutional right of assembly ought to protect activities that are unreasonable from the perspective of the existing order."

FREEDOM OF ASSEMBLY AND THE INTERNET

Many people feel the Internet will save freedom of assembly. And indeed, the Internet has given new life to this First Amendment freedom by making organizing as easy as booting up your computer. Almost instantly, today's activist can be connected to thousands, even millions, of like-minded people. An organizer can provide information on a cause; keep people up-to-date on political events; and send the location, date, and time of a physical meeting or rally.

President Barack Obama's 2008 presidential victory, which resulted from the first Internet campaign in history, is proof of the Internet's effectiveness in assembling and organizing for a cause. According to the Pew Research Center, during the 2008 campaign, 74 percent of Internet users (55 percent of all adults) used the

President Barack Obama's 2008 presidential campaign was the first campaign organized and run using the Internet. Above, a woman watches a videotaped message on Obama's Presidential Exploratory Committee Web site on January 16, 2007.

Internet to get news and information, post their own thoughts, watch videos, share information with others, and engage in political debate. Both Obama and his opponent, John McCain, used the Internet, but Obama's campaign was much more effective. Sarah Lai Stirland, on Wired.com, notes that Obama volunteers organized one hundred fifty thousand events during the entire campaign plus another one thousand phone-banking events during the week before the election. His supporters created more than thirty-fve thousand Web sites, and the campaign raised $600 million from three million contributors, with many of them donating online.

But can the Internet really replace assemblies in physical locations? And should it? People still seek opportunities to practice their free-expression rights outdoors in public spaces. These spaces are still the most reliable venue of expression for poor people and poorly financed causes. Speakers in public spaces cannot be ignored or deleted, and they are much likelier to receive media coverage outdoors than online. Outdoor listeners cannot avoid or filter out contrary or dissenting views as they can online. Plus, a physical assembly where people can see and interact generates emotion and solidarity that cannot be duplicated online. In person, activists can not only reach an audience but can interact with and seek to persuade others directly. Throughout our history, people have stood up for causes by standing and marching together.

RESTRICTION OF SPEECH AND ASSEMBLY

The Supreme Court has always restricted speech in public places. By default, these restrictions also affect freedom of assembly, since speech would be irrelevant without a crowd assembled to hear it. Early restrictions were based on the TPM doctrine, that is, the "time, place, and manner" of speech. Time restrictions might prohibit speech after certain hours or in congested areas during rush hour. Place restrictions limit where speech can occur. The Supreme Court has identified "traditional public forums" (primarily parks, sidewalks, and streets) as the only forums where free speech is traditionally allowed. Even here, permits or fees may be required. Manner refers to the way a message is delivered. Often, this is by speech or the written word (for example, leaflets), but in 1989, the Supreme Court ruled that flag burning was symbolic speech and protected by the First Amendment. If restrictions are placed on freedom of speech in public places, alternative methods of communication must be available. In the past, this was usually through pamphlets or leaflets; today it is often the Internet.

The public forum doctrine is a more recent and, some say, an overly restrictive set of regulations. According to the Web site freedomforum.org, the doctrine states that, in a traditional public forum,

Activists in Washington, D.C., protest the reelection of President George W. Bush by burning the American flag on January 20, 2005. Flag burning has been protected by the Constitution as "symbolic speech" since 1989.

"the state may not restrict speech based on content unless it can show that its regulation is necessary to serve a compelling state interest and is narrowly tailored to achieve that interest." In the twenty-first century, government officials—municipal, state, and federal—are finding more "compelling state interests" and thereby restricting freedom of expression more and more.

FREE-SPEECH ZONES

Opportunities for Americans to assemble, speak, and march outdoors are steadily diminishing. Fewer public spaces are available as cities build up and more real estate is occupied by streets or private buildings. But also, due to more restrictive regulations or to police and government actions, speakers are forced to move, often to places far from their intended audiences. Marches may be prevented entirely.

Timothy Zick's book, *Speech Out of Doors*, graphically illustrates how freedom of assembly has changed. At the 2004 Democratic National Convention in Boston, demonstrators wanted to protest outside the convention center. They wanted to be seen and heard by delegates, bystanders, and media. But federal and local officials set up a special Demonstration Zone (later known as the DZ, "cage," or "pen"). The DZ was a shell of barricades and fences surrounded by two thick layers of mesh and topped with razor wire. National Guardsmen were stationed around it to maintain order and "safety." Protesters could not pass out leaflets or hold signs big enough to be seen. Inside the DZ, they would be effectively removed from their intended audience. A federal judge compared the DZ to a prison or an internment camp. Few demonstrators used the DZ, but no judge ever ruled that it violated the First Amendment.

The DZ was an example of an increasingly common trend—the free-speech zone. This is an area set aside in a public space, inside which activists are allowed to practice their freedom of expression (and outside which they cannot practice it). Free-speech zones are not always as shocking as the DZ, but they always separate protesters from their intended audience, thereby diminishing their ability to communicate. In today's world, where governments and citizens fear terrorist attacks, officials often require free-speech zones for "security reasons." But the end result is repression, not expression.

On the flip side of the free-speech zone, federal law also sets up a protective "bubble" or restricted zone, not around the demonstrators but around government officials—the people with whom demonstrators wish to communicate. The Federal Restricted Buildings and Grounds Improvement Act of 2011 (better known as the Trespass Bill) is a slight revision of an earlier bill. It gives police greater authority to arrest any person who ventures too close to government officials or anyone protected by the Secret Service. The revised Trespass Bill was passed after the January 2011 shooting of Congresswoman Gabrielle Giffords and others at an Arizona shopping center, where Giffords was holding a public forum. Many people feel the bill will seriously endanger people's right to assemble. Law professor Ruthann Robson says, "This act has the

Emergency personnel survey the aftermath of the shooting of Congresswoman Gabrielle Giffords and eighteen other people, six of whom died. Giffords was meeting with constituents on January 8, 2011, at this Tucson, Arizona, shopping center.

potential to chill protest." According to a spokesperson for the Partnership for Civil Justice Fund, "This has always been a bad law," and the new version is not that much worse. But there is no question the bill further separates citizens from their elected representatives and makes it easier to arrest protesters.

In other cases, demonstrations are allowed but police actions, including unwarranted arrests, deter people from participating in protests. At the 2004 Republican National Convention in New York City,

1,806 people were arrested and charged with resisting arrest, obstructing governmental administration, and disorderly conduct. After the protesters were detained and fingerprinted, most of the cases were dismissed outright. Only twenty-eight came to trial and only ten protesters were convicted. Donna Lieberman of the New York Civil Liberties Union says the police "over-arrested" based on post-9/11 security concerns. "When law enforcement conflates lawful protest with a national security threat, we as a democracy are in deep trouble," according to Lieberman.

THE FUTURE OF ASSEMBLY

Recent trends suggest leaders consider freedom of assembly less and less important, but citizens do not agree. Demonstrations for a variety of causes still occur regularly, even as police try to prevent them. The Occupy Wall Street movement is a highly visible example. Thousands of protesters converged on Wall Street, the financial center of the United States, in September 2011. This leaderless movement encompassed citizens disillusioned with the country's financial inequality, government and big business corruption, and general mistrust of government and corporate influence on it. Demonstrations lasted for months and ultimately spread to cities and campuses around the country. Protesters set up semipermanent encampments. But, according to sociologist and

New York City police confront an Occupy Wall Street activist on November 15, 2011, as they clear demonstrators from Zuccotti Park, where the movement had begun two months earlier.

Occupy demonstrator Todd Gitlin, "It's now routine for police to disperse Occupy encampments, to confine demonstrators inside metal fences, corral them in plastic, and sequester them in 'free speech zones' far removed from gatherings they want to influence, or denounce, or otherwise communicate with or about."

Every First Amendment freedom is constantly open to interpretation. How it is interpreted depends on historical context (what is happening at the time the right is questioned) and on the beliefs

SHOULD HATE GROUPS HAVE FIRST AMENDMENT RIGHTS?

Members of Westboro Baptist Church in Topeka, Kansas, regularly picket the funerals of fallen U.S. soldiers. They believe deaths in the Iraq and Afghanistan wars are God's punishment for America's tolerance of homosexuality. The church has been labeled a "hate group" by the Anti-Defamation League and the Southern Poverty Law Center. Last year, the Supreme Court ruled that Westboro protests were protected under the First Amendment. But on August 6, 2012, President Barack Obama signed a bill requiring that protests such as Westboro's remain at least 300 feet (92 meters) from military funerals and not occur for two hours before or after the funeral. Counterdemonstrations have occurred at recent Westboro protests. At the Columbia, Missouri, funeral of Army Specialist Sterling Wyatt in July 2012, thousands of red-shirted supporters formed a "human wall" shielding Wyatt's family and their church from the Westboro protesters.

of those interpreting it. One year the Supreme Court may have a relatively liberal majority and interpret a freedom broadly, allowing more individual freedom. Twenty years later, the Court may have a conservative majority and interpret the same law more narrowly, with greater restrictions. All judges are supposed to be impartial. But some people feel that, more and more, the Supreme Court justices' decisions reflect the political views of the president who appointed them. The Honorable John C. Gariglietti, chief judge of Kansas's Eleventh Judicial District, commented, "Now, you know in advance how every justice will vote on any issue—they vote the party line, just as Congress does." Judge Gariglietti did specify one exception—like many, he was surprised by the Court's July 2012 vote upholding the Affordable Care Act.

The bottom line is that citizens must always be alert and continue to fight for their freedoms. Freedoms are not automatically ensured just because they are in the Constitution. Governments will try to restrict individual freedoms, often "for the safety of" or "in the best interest of" citizens. Only an active and engaged citizenry, which constantly uses the freedoms of speech and assembly to make their voices heard, can safeguard those freedoms and ensure they will be available for future generations.

Preamble to the Constitution

We the People of the United States, in order to form a more perfect Union, establish Justice, insure domestic Tranquility, provide for the common defense, promote the general Welfare, and secure the Blessings of Liberty to ourselves and our Posterity, do ordain and establish this Constitution for the United States of America.

On September 25, 1789, Congress transmitted to the state legislatures twelve proposed amendments, two of which, having to do with congressional representation and congressional pay, were not adopted. The remaining ten amendments became the Bill of Rights.

The Bill of Rights

Amendment I

Congress shall make no law respecting an establishment of religion, or prohibiting the free exercise thereof; or abridging the freedom of speech, or of the press; or the right of the people peaceably to assemble, and to petition the Government for a redress of grievances.

Amendment II

A well regulated Militia, being necessary to the security of a free State, the right of the people to keep and bear Arms, shall not be infringed.

Amendment III

No Soldier shall, in time of peace be quartered in any house, without the consent of the Owner, nor in time of war, but in a manner to be prescribed by law.

Amendment IV

The right of the people to be secure in their persons, houses, papers, and effects, against unreasonable searches and seizures, shall not be violated, and no Warrants shall issue, but upon probable cause, supported by Oath or affirmation, and particularly describing the place to be searched, and the persons or things to be seized.

Amendment V

No person shall be held to answer for a capital, or otherwise infamous crime, unless on a presentment or indictment of a Grand Jury, except in cases arising in the land or naval forces, or in the Militia, when in actual service in time of War or public danger; nor shall any person be subject for the same offence to be twice

put in jeopardy of life or limb; nor shall be compelled in any criminal case to be a witness against himself, nor be deprived of life, liberty, or property, without due process of law; nor shall private property be taken for public use, without just compensation.

Amendment VI

In all criminal prosecutions, the accused shall enjoy the right to a speedy and public trial, by an impartial jury of the State and district wherein the crime shall have been committed, which district shall have been previously ascertained by law, and to be informed of the nature and cause of the accusation; to be confronted with the witnesses against him; to have compulsory process for obtaining witnesses in his favor, and to have the Assistance of Counsel for his defense.

Amendment VII

In Suits at common law, where the value in controversy shall exceed twenty dollars, the right of trial by jury shall be preserved, and no fact tried by a jury, shall be otherwise reexamined in any Court of the United States, than according to the rules of the common law.

Amendment VIII

Excessive bail shall not be required, nor excessive fines imposed, nor cruel and unusual punishments inflicted.

Amendment IX

The enumeration in the Constitution, of certain rights, shall not be construed to deny or disparage others retained by the people.

Amendment X

The powers not delegated to the United States by the Constitution, nor prohibited by it to the States, are reserved to the States respectively, or to the people.

abolitionist   Historically, a person who believed in an immediate end to slavery and racial discrimination.

civil disobedience   Deliberately breaking a law to get arrested and bring attention to a cause.

civil rights   Rights to personal liberty and equality, usually considered in reference to minority groups.

disenfranchise   To deprive of a legal right or freedom, such as the right to vote.

free-speech zone   An area set aside in a public place for activists to exercise their right of free speech.

indictment   A formal written statement by a prosecuting attorney charging a person with a crime.

labor union   A group of workers banding together to achieve common goals, such as better working conditions or higher wages; also called a trade union.

lynching   An open public murder carried out by white mobs usually against blacks; occurred in the United States between about 1880 and 1940.

picketing   Standing or marching, usually with a protest sign, near a business or government office; a form of nonviolent protest.

precedent   A court case cited as an example to help decide future cases.

ratify   To sign or formally consent to a contract, treaty, or agreement, making it formally valid.

redress   To remedy or set right.

scab   Derogatory term for a nonunion person who takes a union member's job.

sit-in   An organized nonviolent protest in which participants seat themselves in a place relevant to the protest and refuse to move.

status quo   The existing state of affairs.

strike   An organized event in which workers stop work and refuse to produce until their demands are met.

subversive   Intending to undermine or overthrow an established government.

suffrage   The right to vote.

suffragist   An advocate of extending the right to vote, usually applied to women during the women's suffrage movement.

teach-in   A meeting, usually on a college campus, with lectures, debates, and discussions to raise awareness of a controversial issue.

American Civil Liberties Union

125 Broad Street, 18th Floor

New York, New York 10004

(212) 549-2666

Web site: http://www.aclu.org

The ACLU is dedicated to preserving and defending the liberties provided by the Constitution and laws of the United States. It works in courts, legislatures, and communities to defend First Amendment rights, right of due process, and equal protection under the law and to extend rights to traditionally disenfranchised segments of the population.

Canadian Civil Liberties Association

506 – 360 Bloor Street West

Toronto, ON M5S 1X1

Canada

(416) 363-0321

Web site: http://ccla.org

The CCLA protects human rights and civil liberties of Canadians through public education, citizens' engagement, monitoring, research, and litigation (lawsuits).

Department of Justice Canada

284 Wellington Street

Ottawa, ON K1A 0H8

Canada

(613) 957-4207

Web site: http://www.justice.gc.ca

This Web site contains news and information on the Canadian justice system, including the text of the Canadian Charter of Rights and Freedoms and resources including books and speeches.

FindLaw.com

Web site: http://www.findlaw.com

FindLaw, a major online source for legal information, includes articles and videos on all aspects of the law, including First Amendment rights, and answers citizens' questions about legal problems. It also includes up-to-date legal news stories from around the world and blogs on the law by FindLaw members.

First Amendment Center

John Seigenthaler Center

1207 18th Avenue S

Nashville, TN 37212

(615) 727-1600

Web site: http://www.firstamendmentcenter.org

The First Amendment Center of Vanderbilt University is an educational center and does not give legal advice. It describes itself as "a forum for the study and exploration of freedom-of-expression issues," and includes news articles, lesson plans, and teaching materials, and an annual National First Amendment Moot Court Competition.

National Archives and Records Administration

8601 Adelphi Road

College Park, MD 20740-6001

(866) 272-6272

Web site: http://www.archives.gov/exhibits

The National Archives keeps on file the originals and transcripts of all U.S. documents that are important for historical or legal reasons. It includes the Declaration of Independence, U.S. Constitution, Bill of Rights, and Emancipation Proclamation, as well as the English Magna Carta, plus articles about each document.

The Oyez Project

U.S. Supreme Court Media, IIT Chicago-Kent College
   of Law

Illinois Institute of Technology

565 West Adams Street

Chicago, IL 60661-3691

(312) 906-5000

Web site: http://www.oyez.org

The Oyez Project covers every Supreme Court case since 1953, including short descriptions of each case, the ruling, how each Supreme Court justice ruled on it, and who wrote the concurring and dissenting decisions. The site also includes a multimedia section containing audio of Supreme Court proceedings and a virtual tour of the Supreme Court building. Two smart phone apps are also available: PocketJustice and OyezToday.

WEB SITES

Due to the changing nature of Internet links, Rosen Publishing has developed an online list of Web sites related to the subject of this book. This site is updated regularly. Please use this link to access the list:

http://www.rosenlinks.com/PFCD/RTA

Brownell, Richard. *Counterculture of the 1960s* (World History). Farmington Hills, MI: Lucent Books, 2010.

Campbell, Heather M. *The Britannica Guide to Political and Social Movements That Changed the Modern World* (Turning Points in History). New York, NY: Rosen Educational Services, 2009.

Dougherty, Terri. *Freedom of Expression and the Internet* (Hot Topics). Farmington Hills, MI: Lucent Books. 2010.

Haynes, Charles C., Sam Chaltain, and Susan M. Glisson. *First Freedoms: A Documentary History of First Amendment Rights in America.* New York, NY: Oxford University Press USA, 2006.

Jacobs, Thomas A. *Teens Take It to Court: Young People Who Challenged the Law—and Changed Your Life.* Minneapolis, MN: Free Spirit Publishing, 2006.

Jones, Clarence B., and Stuart Connelly. *Behind the Dream: The Making of the Speech That Transformed a Nation.* New York, NY: Palgrave Macmillan, 2011.

Kline, Benjamin. *First Along the River: A Brief History of the U.S. Environmental Movement.* Lanham, MD: Rowman & Littlefield Publishers, 2011.

Lane, Charles. *The Day Freedom Died: The Colfax Massacre, the Supreme Court, and the Betrayal of Reconstruction.* New York, NY: Holt Paperbacks, 2009.

Lerner, Adrienne. *Freedom of Expression* (Global Viewpoints). Farmington Hills, MI: Greenhaven Press, 2009.

Marsico, Katie. *Women's Right to Vote: America's Suffrage Movement* (Perspectives On). New York, NY: Benchmark Books, 2010.

Merino, Noel. *Freedom of Assembly and Association* (Teen Rights and Freedoms). Farmington Hills, MI: Greenhaven Press, 2012.

Merino, Noel, ed. *Free Speech and Expression* (Teen Rights and Freedoms). Farmington Hills, MI: Greenhaven Press, 2011.

Patrick, John J. *The Bill of Rights: A History in Documents* (Pages from History). New York, NY: Oxford University Press USA, 2003.

Qualey, Marsha. *Come In from the Cold.* New York, NY: Houghton Mifflin Graphia, 2008.

Rohde, Stephen F. *Freedom of Assembly* (American Rights). New York, NY: Facts On File, Inc., 2005.

Sloman, Des. *The Call: A Novel Set in the 1960s and 1970s During the Time of the Vietnam War.* LaVergne, TN: Stategic Book Publishing, 2012.

Winters, Robert, ed. *Freedom of Assembly and Petition* (The Bill of Rights). Farmington Hills, MI: Greenhaven Press, 2006.

Zott, Lynn. *The Arab Spring* (Opposing Viewpoints). Farmington Hills, MI: Greenhaven Press, 2012.

Abernathy, M. Glenn. *The Right of Assembly and Association*. 2nd Edition, Revised. Columbia, SC: University of South Carolina Press, 1981, pp. 11-16.

American Civil Liberties Union. "Free Speech Under Fire: The ACLU Challenge to 'Protest Zones.'" September 23, 2003. Retrieved July 22, 2012 (http://www.aclu.org/free-speech/free-speech-under -fire-aclu-challenge-protest-zones).

Barringer, Mark. "The Anti-War Movement in the United States." From *Encyclopedia of the Vietnam War: A Political, Social, and Military History*. Edited by Spencer C. Tucker. Oxford, England: ABC-CLIO, 1998. Retrieved August 2, 2012 (http://www.english .illinois.edu/maps/vietnam/antiwar.html).

Bill of Rights Institute. "Freedom of Speech–Skokie and Brandenburg." 2010. Retrieved July 23, 2012 (http://billofrightsinstitute.org/resources).

Bovard, James. "Free-Speech Zone." The American Conservative, December 15, 2003. Retrieved July 22, 2012 (http://www.theamericanconservative .com/articles/free-speech-zone).

First Amendment Schools, First Amendment Center. "Assembly. Frequently Asked Questions." 2012. Retrieved July 18, 2012 (http://www.firstamendment schools.org/freedoms/assemblyfaqs.aspx).

Gans, David H. "This Day in Supreme Court History: *United States v. Cruikshank*."

BIBLIOGRAPHY

Constitutional Accountability Center, March 27, 2009. Retrieved July 21, 2012 (https://theus constitution.org/text-history/580).

History.com. "Red Scare." Retrieved July 27, 2012 (http://www.history.com/topics/red-scare).

History.com. "Vietnam War Protests." Retrieved August 2, 2012 (http://www.history.com/topics/vietnam-war-protests).

Illinois First Amendment Center. "First Amendment Research Information: Court Cases–Right to Peaceably Assemble." 2012. Retrieved May 29, 2012 (http://www.illinoisfirstamendmentcenter.com/research_CourtCases_RightToPeaceableAssem.php).

Inazu, John D. "The Forgotten Freedom of Assembly." *Tulane Law Review*, 2010. Retrieved May 29, 2012 (http://scholarship.law.duke.edu/faculty_scholarship/2116).

Lewis, Jerry M., and Thomas R. Hensley. "The May 4 Shootings at Kent State University: The Search for Historical Accuracy." *The Ohio Council for the Social Studies Review*. Retrieved 2012 (http://dept.kent.edu/sociology/lewis/lewihen.htm).

McIntire, Richard J. "Impacting Change–Students in the Civil Rights Movement." *The Black Collegian Online Archives*. Retrieved July 31, 2012 (http://www.black-collegian.com/issues/2ndsem08).

Meyer, David S. *The Politics of Protest: Social Movements in America*. New York, NY: Oxford University Press, 2007.

National Archives. The Charters of Freedom. "Bill of Rights." Retrieved June 10, 2012 (http://www .archives.gov/exhibits/charters/bill_of_rights.html).

National Archives. The Charters of Freedom. "Constitution of the United States: A History." Retrieved June 10, 2012 (http://www.archives. gov/exhibits/charters/constitution_history.html).

National Organization for Women. "History of Marches and Mass Actions." Retrieved July 18, 2012 (http://www.now.org/history/protests.html).

The Oyez Project at IIT Chicago-Kent College of Law. Retrieved July 22, 2012 (http://www.oyez .org/cases).

Russell, Margaret M., ed. *Freedom of Assembly and Petition (The First Amendment): Its Constitutional History and the Contemporary Debate*. Amherst, NY: Prometheus Books, 2010.

Walton, Mary. *A Woman's Crusade. Alice Paul and the Battle for the Ballot*. New York, NY: Palgrave Macmillan, 2010.

Zick, Timothy. *Speech Out of Doors: Preserving First-Amendment Liberties in Public Places*. New York, NY: Cambridge University Press, 2008.

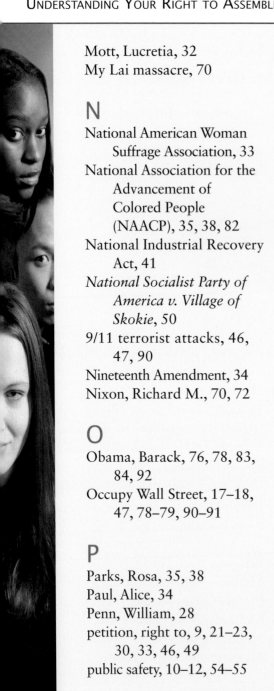

About the Author

Carol Hand has a Ph.D. in zoology. She has taught college biology, written assessments and curricula for the middle and high school levels, and authored a number of young adult books on science and social studies. As a child of the sixties, she has firsthand knowledge of the importance of First Amendment rights, including freedom of assembly, and has followed the exercise of that right through the years.

Photo Credits

Cover, pp. 1, 3, 9, 26, 48, 66, 80 Monika Graff/Getty Images; pp. 4–5 DEA Picture Library/De Agostini/Getty Images; pp. 10–11 Scott Olson/Getty Images; p. 15 iStockphoto/Thinkstock; pp. 18–19 Underwood Archives/Archive Photos/Getty Images; p. 20 Emmanuel Dunand/AFP/Getty Images; p. 25 Universal Images Group/Getty Images; pp. 27, 86–87 Mario Tama/Getty Images; p. 29 Stock Montage/Archive Photos/Getty Images; pp. 31, 40–41 Library of Congress Prints and Photographs Division; pp. 36–37 Robert Abbott Sengstacke/Archive Photos/Getty Images; pp. 44–45 Alex Wong/Getty Images; pp. 48–49 The Washington Post/Getty Images; pp. 52–53 http://en.wikipedia.org/wiki/File:Colfax_Riot_sign_IMG_2401.JPG CCBY 3.0; pp. 58–59, 60–61, 64 © AP Images; p. 67 Archive Photos/Getty Images; pp. 68–69 Art Shay/Time & Life Pictures/Getty Images; pp. 74–75 Mandel Ngan/AFP/Getty Images; pp. 76–77 Justin Sullivan/Getty Images; p. 81 Spencer Platt/Getty Images; pp. 83, 86, 89 Karen Bleier/AFP/Getty Images; p. 91 James Palka/Getty Images; page and text box border images © iStockphoto.com/Wayne Howard (crowd & flag), © iStockphoto.com/DHuss (U. S. Capitol building), © iStockphoto.com/Andrea Gingerich (faces).

Designer: Les Kanturek; Editor: Bethany Bryan;
Photo Researcher: Amy Feinberg